I LOVE MY BABY BERIMBAU:
An Introduction to the Berimbau in Capoeira

Written by Dr. Daphnie Bruno

Illustrated by Clarice Manning

Elevated Living Publishing

Elevated Living Publishing

Printed in the United States of America

First Printing: February 2011

Dedicated to Sela Yasmin my capoeira baby

I acknowledge all of the divine forces that inspired my work. All my family and friends who pushed me forward to get this done. To Clarice, your art brought my visions and words to so much depth.
To Donna Hinton, thank you for editing the book.

Thank you.

I LOVE MY BABY BERIMBAU,
I LOVE ALL **ITS** SPECIAL PARTS.

THE DOBRAO, BAQUETA AND CAXIXI HELP MAKE THE SOUND UNIQUE.

THERE IS ALSO THE CABASA, ARAME, CORDAO AND VERGA.

PUTTING THEM TOGETHER IS SO MUCH FUN FOR ME.

I LOVE MY BABY BERIMBAU,
I LOVE THE WAY IT LOOKS.

I LOVE THE WAY IT CURVES AND BENDS AND EVEN THE WAY IT IS HELD.

I LOVE MY BABY BERIMBAU,
I LOVE THE SOUNDS YOU SEE.

IN THE GAME OF CAPOEIRA
IT IS THE INSTRUMENT THAT
MOVES ME.

I LOVE MY BABY BERIMBAU,
IT IS SPECIAL YOU WILL SEE.

IT WILL TAKE YOU TO A
SPECIAL PLACE WHERE YOU
WILL ALWAYS WANT TO BE.

GLOSSARY OF TERMS

CAPOEIRA:
AFRO-BRAZILIAN GAME AND ART FORM USED BY ENSLAVED AFRICANS TO
FREE THEMSELVES FROM COLONIAL OPPRESSION. TODAY CAPOEIRA IS
PLAYED IN NEARLY EVERY CONTINENT AS A FORM OF MARTIAL ART THAT
EMPOWERS AND CONNECTS INDIVIDUALS BACK TO AFRICAN CULTURE.

DOBRAO (COIN):
OLD BRAZILIAN COIN USED
TO PLAY A BERIMBAU

ARAME (WIRE):
THE WIRE THAT THE VEGETA
STRIKES TO MAKE THE SOUND

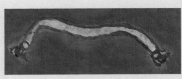
CORDAO (CORD):
THE STRING THAT ATTATCHES THE GOURD
TO THE BERIMBAU. IT ALSO KEEPS THE ARAME
ATTACHED TO THE VERGA

CAXIX (SHAKER):
A RATTLE FILLED WITH EITHER ROCKS OR COWRIE SHELLS THAT IS USUALLY PLAYED WITH THE BERIMBAU

CABASA (GOURD):
THE GOURD WHERE THE SOUND OF THE ARAME IS MADE LOUDER

BAQUETA (STICK):
A STICK USED TO STRIKE THE WIRE OF A BERIMBAU

VERGA (BOW):
THE LONG PIECE OF WOOD
THE ARAME IS ATTACHED TO.

BERIMBAU:
ONE-STRINGED PRECUSSION INSTRUMENT
RESEMBLING A BOW

BARIBA:
WOOD USED FOR MAKING THE VERGA
OF A BERIMBAU

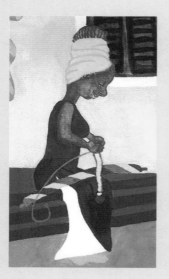

MESTRE (MASTER):
ONE WHO HAS MASTERED THE
ART OF CAPOEIRA

RODA:
A CIRCLE OF PEOPLE IN WHICH
CAPOEIRA IS PLAYED

ABOUT THE AUTHOR

Born in Cabaret, Haiti, Daphnie Bruno migrated to Brooklyn, New York as a young child. While completing her doctorate at Howard University, Dr. Bruno fell in love with Capoeira, the Afro-Brazilian martial arts. It is this love for Capoeira that has inspired this current children's book. Dr. Bruno is an advocate for culturally appropriate text in education. Through research, writing and teaching, Dr. Bruno hopes to shed light into the various factors that contribute to healthy black child development. Dr. Bruno is also an inspirational speaker and continues to empower the politically and economically disadvantaged groups. She is available for speaking engagements and can be contacted at daphniebruno@yahoo.com

ABOUT THE ILLUSTRATOR

Born and raised in Washington DC, Clarice Manning lives for her passion in expressing herself through art. Clarice received her Bachelor's Degree of Visual Communications from Gibbs College in Vienna, Virginia. Past projects include murals for the Universal Capoeira Angola Center and various advertising material for people within the DC community. Working with many different art forms this book is her first debut to creating fun and enlightening illustrations for children to enjoy. Her other pass time interests include henna body art, summer festivals and training the art of capoeira angola.